brownie bliss

brownie bliss

Linda Collister

RYLAND
PETERS
& SMALL

LONDON NEW YORK

First published in the
United Kingdom in 2010
by Ryland Peters & Small
20-21 Jockey's Fields
London WC1R 4BW
www.rylandpeters.com

The recipes in this book were
previously published in *Brownies*
and *Christmas Treats to Make
and Give*.

10 9 8 7 6 5 4 3 2 1

ISBN: 978 1 84975 028 8

A CIP record for this book is
available from the British Library.

Printed in China

Senior Designer Iona Hoyle
Senior Commissioning Editor
Julia Charles
Production Gordana Simakovic
Art Director Leslie Harrington
Publishing Director Alison Starling

Food Stylists Linda Tubby and
Rachel Miles
Prop Stylists Roísín Nield and
Liz Belton
Index Hilary Bird

Notes
• All spoon measurements are
level unless otherwise specified.
• Ovens should be preheated
to the specified temperatures.
All ovens work slightly differently.
I recommend using an oven
thermometer and suggest you
consult the maker's handbook
for any special instructions
particularly if you are using a
fan-assisted oven as you may
need to adjust cooking
temperatures according to
manufacturer's instructions.

contents

a little bite of heaven

Chocolate brownies are both homely and decadent. They are quick and easy to put together, yet immensely rich and satisfying. So what makes a brownie different from cake? The texture is crucial; a good brownie should be soft, with a close, moist, fudgy quality completely unlike the crumbly, open and light texture of a sponge cake. For this reason it is always far better to undercook brownies slightly, than to overcook them.

It's well worth using the best quality chocolate you can find – choose bars made with around 70 per cent cocoa solids which will give a good depth of flavour. Cocoa powder is also often added to increase the intensity of flavour without adding more sugar. The same applies to white chocolate – use very good quality for a deep flavour rather than a cloying sweetness.

I've included old-fashioned brownies plus some new ones that may shock the purists! Although the 'classic' brownies use pecans or walnuts, many of these recipes are nut-free. Some are 'grown-up' brownies with a dash of Kirsch or rum, some are muffins for lunchboxes and, because I like to serve brownies at the end of a meal, I've included some recipes that make delicious desserts along with sauces to serve with them. But, all you really need is a glass of cold milk or a hot cup of coffee and a square of freshly-baked brownie, warm from the oven.

making a classic brownie

If you've never made brownies before, this easy recipe for a Classic Fudge Brownie will get you hooked. It's the first one I ever made and it's a winner! Eat it warm from the oven with a scoop of vanilla ice cream and plenty of hot chocolate sauce.

classic fudge brownie

100 g dark chocolate

125 g unsalted butter, softened

275 g caster sugar

1 teaspoon vanilla extract

2 large eggs, lightly beaten

85 g plain flour

2 tablespoons unsweetened cocoa powder

100 g pecan halves or pieces

50 g dark chocolate, roughly chopped or dark choc chips

a 23-cm square brownie tin or similar, greased and base-lined

Makes 20

Preheat the oven to 180°C (350°F) Gas 4.

Break the 100 g of chocolate into pieces and put it in a heatproof bowl. Set the bowl over a pan of steaming water and melt the chocolate gently, stirring frequently. Do not let the base of the bowl touch the water. Remove the bowl from the pan and set aside until needed.

Put the butter in a large mixing bowl and use either a wooden spoon or a hand-held electric mixer to beat until soft and creamy. Add the sugar and vanilla extract and continue beating until the mixture is soft and fluffy. Gradually beat in the eggs then beat in the melted chocolate.

Sift the flour and cocoa directly onto the mixture and stir in. When thoroughly combined add the nuts and the chopped chocolate and stir in. Transfer the mixture to the prepared tin, spread evenly and level the surface.

Bake in the preheated oven for about 25-30 minutes until a skewer inserted in the centre comes out just clean. Remove the tin from the oven.

Leave to cool in the tin until just warm before removing and cutting into 20 pieces. Best eaten warm. Once cold, store in an airtight container and eat within 5 days.

everyday brownies

Some enthusiasts believe that only cocoa should be used in a classic brownie, not melted chocolate, as it gives a deeper, truly intense flavour which balances the sugar necessary to give a proper fudgy texture. Choose the best quality cocoa you can find.

old-fashioned brownies

Preheat the oven to 170°C (325°F) Gas 3.

Put the walnut pieces in an ovenproof dish and lightly toast in the preheated oven for about 10 minutes. Remove from the oven and leave to cool. Don't turn off the oven.

Meanwhile break the eggs into a mixing bowl. Use a hand-held electric mixer to whisk them until frothy then whisk in the sugar. Whisk for a minute then, still whisking constantly, add the melted butter in a steady stream. Whisk for 1 further minute then add the vanilla extract.

Sift the flour and cocoa directly into the bowl and stir in with a wooden spoon. When thoroughly combined stir in the toasted walnuts. Transfer the mixture to the prepared tin, spread evenly and level the surface.

Bake in the preheated oven for about 25 minutes until a skewer inserted in the centre comes out just clean. Remove the tin from the oven.

Leave the brownie to cool completely in the tin before removing and cutting into 16 pieces. Store in an airtight container and eat within 5 days.

100 g walnut pieces

4 large eggs

300 g caster sugar

140 g unsalted butter, melted

½ teaspoon vanilla extract

140 g plain flour

75 g unsweetened cocoa powder

a 23-cm square brownie tin or similar, greased and base-lined

Makes 16

There's a lot of chocolate in this recipe, but it's not too sweet due to the high cocoa content and the addition of either walnut or pecan pieces. These brownies are particularly good eaten warm as a dessert with a little whipped cream on the side.

very rich brownies

Preheat the oven to 180°C (350°F) Gas 4.

Break up the chocolate and put it in a heatproof bowl. Set the bowl over a pan of steaming water and gently melt the chocolate, stirring frequently. Do not let the base of the bowl touch the water. Remove the bowl from the pan and leave to cool until needed.

Put the soft butter and sugar in a mixing bowl and use either a wooden spoon or a hand-held electric mixer to beat until fluffy. Gradually beat in the eggs then add the vanilla extract. Next, beat in the melted chocolate. When thoroughly combined sift the flour and cocoa directly onto the mixture and stir in. Mix in the nuts then transfer the mixture to the prepared tin, spread evenly and level the surface.

Bake in the preheated oven for about 20 minutes until almost firm to the touch. Remove the tin from the oven.

Leave to cool in the tin before removing, cutting into 20 pieces and sprinkling with chocolate shavings. (These can be made by grating dark chocolate using the coarse hole side of a grater.) Serve with whipped cream, if liked. Store in an airtight container and eat within 4 days.

200 g dark chocolate

100 g unsalted butter, softened

250 g light muscovado sugar

4 large eggs, lightly beaten

½ teaspoon vanilla extract

60 g plain flour

60 g unsweetened cocoa powder

100 g walnut or pecan pieces

dark chocolate shavings, to decorate

whipped cream, to serve (optional)

a 23-cm square brownie tin or similar, greased and base-lined

Makes 20

Walnuts have a creamy, bittersweet taste that contrasts well with the sweetness of the brownie mixture. Here, there is a high proportion of walnuts to mixture, plus a fudgy walnut topping. For a deeper flavour, toast the nuts for 10 minutes in the oven before adding to both the brownie and topping mixtures.

extra-nutty brownies

Preheat the oven to 180°C (350°F) Gas 4.

Put the chocolate in a heatproof mixing bowl with the butter. Set the bowl over a pan of steaming water and melt gently, stirring frequently. Do not let the base of the bowl touch the water.

Remove the bowl from the pan and stir in the sugar and vanilla extract. Add the eggs and use a wooden spoon or hand-held electric mixer to beat well until the mixture comes together as a smooth batter. Sift the flour and cocoa directly into the bowl and stir in. When combined stir in the nuts (reserving about 50 g to top). Transfer the mixture to the prepared tin, spread evenly and level the surface.

Bake in the preheated oven for about 15 minutes until just firm to the touch. Remove the tin from the oven. Leave to cool completely in the tin before carefully removing.

Meanwhile make the frosting: melt the chocolate and butter as above. Remove the bowl from the pan and stir in the milk. Sift the cocoa and icing sugar into the bowl and mix in. When the frosting is thick and smooth spread it over the cooled brownie. Push the reserved walnut pieces into the frosting to finish.

Once the topping is firm, cut into 20 pieces. Store in an airtight container and eat within 4 days.

100 g dark chocolate, chopped

115 g unsalted butter

200 g light muscovado sugar

½ teaspoon vanilla extract

2 large eggs, lightly beaten

100 g plain flour

2 tablespoons unsweetened cocoa powder

200 g walnut pieces

Frosting:

50 g dark chocolate

50 g unsalted butter

2 tablespoons full-fat milk

2 tablespoons unsweetened cocoa powder

100 g icing sugar

a 23-cm square brownie tin or similar, greased and base-lined

Makes 20

Chocolate and peanuts is a classic combination. This recipe is included by popular demand from my American family. I always use a top-quality peanut butter with no added sugar or fat as it gives by far the best flavour.

peanut butter brownies

100 g dark chocolate

175 g unsalted butter, diced

3 large eggs

200 g light muscovado sugar

120 g plain flour

2 tablespoons unsweetened cocoa powder

Peanut mixture:

180 g smooth peanut butter

50 g caster sugar

1 tablespoon plain flour

5 tablespoons full-fat milk

2 tablespoons unsalted roasted peanuts

a 23-cm square brownie tin or similar, greased and base-lined

Makes 16

Preheat the oven to 180°C (350°F) Gas 4.

Break up the chocolate and put it in a heatproof bowl with the butter. Set the bowl over a pan of steaming water and melt gently, stirring frequently. Do not let the base of the bowl touch the water. Remove the bowl from the pan and set aside until needed.

Break the eggs into a mixing bowl and use a hand-held electric mixer to beat well. Add the sugar and whisk until the mixture is very thick and mousse-like in texture.

Whisk in the melted chocolate mixture. Sift the flour and cocoa directly onto the mixture and mix until thoroughly combined. Transfer the mixture to the prepared tin, spread evenly and level the surface.

Put all the ingredients for the peanut mixture into a separate bowl and mix well. Drop teaspoonfuls of this mixture, evenly spaced, onto the chocolate mixture. Use the end of a chopstick or teaspoon handle to marble or swirl both mixtures. Scatter the peanuts over the top.

Bake in the preheated oven for about 30 minutes until just firm. Leave to cool in the tin before removing and cutting into 16 pieces. Store in an airtight container and eat within 5 days.

A simple all-in-one recipe that owes its lovely, intense flavour to dark chocolate flavoured with good, strong coffee. This chocolate is most often sold in bars labelled as 'espresso chocolate'.

easy mocha brownies

Preheat the oven to 180°C (350°F) Gas 4.

Break up the chocolate and put it in a heatproof bowl with the butter. Set the bowl over a pan of steaming water and leave to melt gently, stirring very frequently. Do not let the base of the bowl touch the water.

Remove the bowl from the pan and stir in the sugar. Stir in the beaten eggs. When thoroughly combined stir in the flour, then finally mix in the nuts. Transfer the mixture to the prepared tin and spread evenly.

Bake in the preheated oven for about 25-30 minutes until a skewer inserted in the centre comes out just clean. Remove the tin from the oven.

Leave to cool in the tin before removing and cutting into 9 pieces. Store in an airtight container and eat within 5 days.

100 g dark 'espresso' chocolate

175 g unsalted butter, diced

225 g caster sugar

3 large eggs, lightly beaten

50 g plain flour

150 g walnut pieces

a 23-cm square brownie tin or similar, greased and base-lined

Makes 9

There are no nuts but plenty of chocolate in these moist, rich brownies. For the most intense flavour, use top-quality white and dark chocolate.

triple chocolate brownies

200 g dark chocolate, chopped

100 g unsalted butter, at room temperature, diced

225 g caster sugar

½ teaspoon vanilla extract

4 large eggs

60 g plain flour

60 g unsweetened cocoa powder

100 g white chocolate, coarsely chopped

a 23-cm square brownie tin or similar, greased and base-lined

Makes 24

Preheat the oven to 180°C (350°F) Gas 4.

Melt the chocolate in a heatproof bowl set over a pan of steaming water and stir occasionally until melted. Do not let the base of the bowl touch the water. Remove the bowl from the heat and set aside until needed.

Put the butter, sugar and vanilla extract in a mixing bowl and use a wooden spoon or hand-held electric mixer to beat until light and fluffy. Gradually beat in the eggs, beating well after each addition. Stir in the melted chocolate, then sift the flour and cocoa directly into the bowl and mix in.

Transfer the mixture to the prepared tin, spread evenly and level the surface. Scatter the chopped white chocolate over the top.

Bake in the preheated oven for about 20 minutes until a skewer inserted in the centre comes out slightly moist but not sticky with uncooked batter. Remove the tin from the oven.

Leave to cool completely in the tin before cutting into 24 pieces. Store in an airtight container and eat within 4 days.

I'm often asked for a brownie recipe without flour, and this one is quite wonderful. It is incredibly rich and sticky, and is perfect served with a scoop of vanilla ice cream. As with many chocolate cakes, it is at its best made a day in advance.

flourless sticky brownies

Preheat the oven to 180°C (350°F) Gas 4.

Put the chocolate and butter in a heatproof bowl set over a pan of steaming water and stir frequently until melted. Do not let the base of the bowl touch the water. Remove the bowl from the heat and set aside until needed.

Put the eggs and sugar in a mixing bowl and use a hand-held electric mixer to whisk until very pale, thick and mousse-like in texture.

Using a large metal spoon, fold in the melted chocolate mixture. Combine the ground almonds with the baking powder and mix in, followed by the walnuts.

Transfer the mixture to the prepared tin, spread evenly and level the surface. Bake in the preheated oven for about 40 minutes until just firm to touch and a skewer inserted in the centre comes out clean. Remove the tin from the oven.

Leave to cool completely in the tin before cutting into 24 pieces, or if possible, wrap the entire brownie in foil or greaseproof paper and leave for a day before cutting. Serve with ice cream, if liked. Store in an airtight container and eat within 5 days.

300 g dark chocolate, chopped

225 g unsalted butter, diced

3 large eggs

225 g light muscovado sugar

75 g ground almonds

1 teaspoon baking powder

100 g walnut pieces

vanilla ice cream, to serve (optional)

a 23-cm square brownie tin or similar, greased and base-lined

Makes 24

special brownies

These dark, double-chocolate brownies have a light texture and are subtly flavoured with rum. Serve them with a scoop of vanilla ice cream on top and a drizzle of hot chocolate sauce for a deliciously grown-up dessert.

choc choc rum brownies

Preheat the oven to 180°C (350°F) Gas 4.

Break up the 60 g dark chocolate and put it in a heatproof bowl. Set the bowl over a pan of steaming water and melt gently, stirring frequently. Do not let the base of the bowl touch the water. Remove the bowl from the pan and set aside until needed.

Put the soft butter and icing sugar in a mixing bowl and beat with a wooden spoon or hand-held electric mixer until light and creamy.

Gradually beat in the eggs, followed by the rum. Scrape down the sides then beat in the melted chocolate. Stir in the flour, and when thoroughly combined, add the chopped chocolate and the nuts and mix thoroughly. Transfer the mixture to the prepared tin, spread evenly and level the surface.

Bake in the preheated oven for about 20–25 minutes until the top is set and firm. Leave to cool a little in the tin before removing (taking care as the crust is fragile) and cutting into 16 pieces.

Serve warm or at room temperature with ice cream and hot sauce, if liked. Once cool, store in an airtight container and eat within 4 days.

60 g dark chocolate

85 g unsalted butter, softened

200 g icing sugar

2 large eggs, lightly beaten

2 tablespoons dark rum

60 g plain flour

100 g dark chocolate, finely chopped or dark choc chips

50 g walnut pieces

vanilla ice cream and hot Creamy Chocolate Sauce (see page 63), to serve

a 23-cm square brownie tin or similar, greased and base-lined

Makes 16

The sharpness of dried cranberries balances the sweetness of this dark chocolate brownie mixture, and the tangy grated orange zest lifts the richness. The combinations of flavours makes this an ideal treat during the festive season.

cranberry & dark chocolate brownies

200 g dark chocolate

200 g unsalted butter, diced

3 large eggs

175 g caster sugar

finely grated zest of 1 medium unwaxed orange

200 g plain flour

100 g dried cranberries

a 23-cm square brownie tin or similar, greased and base-lined

Makes 20

Preheat the oven to 180°C (350°F) Gas 4.

Break up the chocolate and put it in a heatproof mixing bowl with the butter. Set the bowl over a pan of steaming water and melt gently, stirring frequently. Do not let the base of the bowl touch the water. Remove the bowl from the pan and set aside until needed.

Break the eggs into a mixing bowl and use a hand-held electric mixer to whisk until frothy. Add the sugar and orange zest and whisk until the mixture becomes very thick and mousse-like in texture. Whisk in the melted chocolate mixture.

Sift the flour directly onto the mixture and stir in. When thoroughly combined stir in the dried cranberries. Transfer the mixture to the prepared tin, spread evenly and level the surface.

Bake in the preheated oven for about 25 minutes until a skewer inserted in the centre comes out just clean. Remove the tin from the oven.

Leave to cool in the tin before removing and cutting into 20 pieces. Store in an airtight container and eat within 5 days.

This brownie is rich and fudgy with masses of chocolate, plus a good shot of strong espresso coffee to offset the sweetness. Serve with a little chilled pouring cream and you have an elegant dinner party dessert.

espresso brownies

Preheat the oven to 180°C (350°F) Gas 4.

Break up the chocolate and put it in a heatproof bowl. Set the bowl over a pan of steaming water and melt gently, stirring frequently. Do not let the base of the bowl touch the water. Remove the bowl from the pan and set aside until needed.

Put the soft butter and sugar in a mixing bowl and use a wooden spoon or hand-held electric mixer to beat until light and fluffy. Gradually beat in the eggs, then the coffee.

Sift the flour and cocoa into the bowl and stir in. Add the melted chocolate and mix in. When thoroughly combined transfer the mixture to the prepared tin, spread evenly and level the surface.

Bake in the preheated oven for about 25 minutes until a skewer inserted in the centre comes out just clean. Remove the tin from the oven.

Leave to cool in the tin for 10 minutes before lightly dusting with cocoa powder, removing and cutting into 20 pieces. Serve warm or at room temperature with cream for pouring, if liked. Once cool, store in an airtight container and eat within 5 days.

230 g dark chocolate

115 g unsalted butter, softened

300 g caster sugar

5 large eggs, lightly beaten

4 tablespoons freshly brewed strong espresso coffee, at room temperature

70 g plain flour

70 g unsweetened cocoa powder, plus a little extra for dusting

single cream, to serve (optional)

a 23-cm square brownie tin or similar, greased and base-lined

Makes 20

This recipe is for my husband, who came across these unusual brownies in a San Francisco deli and begged me to make them for him at home. You'll need a box (or bar) of bittersweet dark chocolate with a soft, mint-flavoured fondant centre, of the type that is most often sold as 'after-dinner' mints.

choc-mint brownies

Preheat the oven to 180°C (350°F) Gas 4.

125 g dark chocolate

100 g unsalted butter, diced

3 large eggs

200 g caster sugar

100 g plain flour

2 tablespoons unsweetened cocoa powder

100 g–200 g bittersweet dark chocolate with mint centre (depending on strength of mint flavour required)

a 23-cm square brownie tin or similar, greased and base-lined

Makes 20

Break up the dark chocolate and put it in a heatproof bowl with the butter. Set the bowl over a pan of steaming water and melt gently, stirring frequently. Do not let the base of the bowl touch the water. Remove the bowl from the pan and set aside until needed.

Break the eggs into a mixing bowl and use a hand-held electric mixer to beat. Add the sugar and whisk until thick and mousse-like in texture.

Whisk in the melted chocolate mixture. Sift the flour and cocoa directly onto the mixture and stir in. When thoroughly combined spoon half the brownie mixture into the prepared tin, spread evenly and level the surface.

Leave the mint chocolates whole or break them up (depending on the size of the ones you are using). Arrange them over the brownie mixture already in the tin. Spoon the remaining brownie mixture on top and gently spread to cover the chocolate mints.

Bake in the preheated oven for about 25 minutes until a skewer inserted in the centre comes out just clean (though some of the sticky mint fondant may appear). Remove the tin from the oven.

Leave to cool in the tin before removing and cutting into 20 pieces. Store in an airtight container and eat within 5 days.

Ginger and chocolate is a delicious taste combination. Here very good dark chocolate flavoured with pieces of crystallized ginger is used in a dark chocolate mixture. Just a hint of spice, plus deliciously tangy soured cream, makes these brownies special.

soured cream & spice brownies

Preheat the oven to 180°C (350°F) Gas 4.

Break up the dark chocolate and put it in a heatproof bowl with the butter. Set the bowl over a pan of steaming water and melt gently, stirring frequently. Do not let the base of the bowl touch the water. Remove the bowl from the pan and set aside until needed.

Put the eggs and sugar in a mixing bowl and use a hand-held electric mixer to whisk until very thick and mousse-like in texture. Whisk in the melted chocolate mixture.

Sift the flour and spices directly into the bowl and stir in. Mix in the soured cream followed by the chopped chocolate with ginger. Transfer the mixture to the prepared tin, spread evenly and level the surface.

Bake in the preheated oven for about 25 minutes until a skewer inserted in the centre comes out just clean. Remove the tin from the oven.

Leave to cool in the tin before removing and cutting into 20 pieces. Store in an airtight container and eat within 5 days.

200 g dark chocolate

100 g unsalted butter

4 large eggs

200 g caster sugar

100 g plain flour

¼ teaspoon ground cinnamon

½ teaspoon ground ginger

3 tablespoons soured cream

50-g bar dark chocolate with crystallized ginger pieces, chopped

a 23-cm square brownie tin or similar, greased and base-lined

Makes 20

Black cherries, Kirsch and dark chocolate are a classic combination. Here, stoned black cherries preserved in a Kirsch syrup are dropped into a well-flavoured, not too sweet, brownie mixture. It makes a perfect dessert for a Christmas or New Year's party, when fruits preserved in alcohol are readily available.

black forest brownies

225 g dark chocolate

125 g unsalted butter, diced

3 tablespoons double cream

3 large eggs

225 g caster sugar

2 tablespoons Kirsch or Kirsch syrup from a jar of cherries

160 g plain flour

100 g dark chocolate, roughly chopped or dark choc chips

465-g jar black cherries in Kirsch (175 g drained weight)

icing sugar, for dusting

whipped cream, to serve

a 23-cm square brownie tin or similar, greased and base-lined

Makes 24

Preheat the oven to 180°C (350°F) Gas 4.

Break up the 225 g chocolate and put it in a heatproof bowl. Add the butter and cream to the bowl and set it over a pan of steaming water. Melt gently, stirring frequently. Do not let the base of the bowl touch the water. Remove the bowl from the pan and set aside until needed.

Break the eggs into a mixing bowl and use a hand-held electric mixer to whisk just until frothy. Add the sugar and Kirsch and whisk until thick and mousse-like in texture. Whisk in the melted chocolate mixture.

Sift the flour directly onto the mixture and stir in. When thoroughly combined stir in the pieces of chocolate. Transfer the mixture to the prepared tin, spread evenly and level the surface. Gently drop the cherries onto the brownie mixture, spacing them as evenly as possible.

Bake in the preheated oven for 30–35 minutes until a skewer inserted in the centre comes out just clean. Remove the tin from the oven.

Leave to cool in the tin before removing and cutting into 24 pieces. Dust lightly with icing sugar just before serving and serve with a dollop of lightly whipped cream on top. Store in an airtight container and eat within 4 days.

These to-die-for brownies are incredibly rich in chocolate and not too sweet. This is a very useful recipe when you need a flour-free dessert or cake. Undercooking is vital to avoid a crumbly texture.

flourless-yet-fudgy brownies

Preheat the oven to 180°C (350°F) Gas 4.

Break up the chocolate and put it in a heatproof bowl with the butter. Set the bowl over a pan of steaming water and melt gently, stirring frequently. Do not let the base of the bowl touch the water. Remove the bowl from the pan and stir in the cocoa. Set aside until needed.

Break the eggs into a mixing bowl and use a hand-held electric mixer to beat well. Add the sugar and whisk thoroughly until very light and frothy and doubled in volume.

Using a large metal spoon, carefully fold in the melted chocolate mixture followed by the nuts. Transfer the mixture to the prepared tin, spread evenly and level the surface.

Bake in the preheated oven for about 25-30 minutes until the top of the brownie is just firm to the touch but the centre is still slightly soft.

Leave to cool in the tin for 10 minutes before carefully removing. Dust lightly with icing sugar before cutting into 12 pieces. Serve warm or at room temperature with a spoonful of soured cream or crème fraîche. Once cool, store in an airtight container and eat within 4 days.

300 g dark chocolate

150 g unsalted butter, diced

50 g unsweetened cocoa powder, sifted

4 large eggs

200 g caster sugar

100 g walnut or pecan pieces

icing sugar, for dusting

soured cream or crème fraîche, to serve

a 23-cm square brownie tin or similar, greased and base-lined

Makes 12

blondies

This blondie recipe from Australia is packed with rich and buttery macadamia nuts. For the best flavour use nuts from a freshly opened pack as they spoil quickly.

macadamia & white chocolate blondies

Preheat the oven to 180°C (350°F) Gas 4.

Break up the 175 g of white chocolate and put it in a heatproof bowl with the butter and set over a pan of steaming water. Melt gently, stirring frequently. Do not let the base of the bowl touch the water.

Remove the bowl from the pan and stir in the sugar with a wooden spoon – don't worry if the mixture looks curdled. Gradually stir in the beaten eggs, then the vanilla extract and beat for a minute until the mixture becomes thick, smooth and glossy.

Sift the flour and baking powder directly onto the mixture and stir in. When thoroughly combined stir in 100 g of the chopped nuts, and the chopped white chocolate.

Transfer the mixture to the prepared tin, spread evenly and level the surface. Scatter the remaining macadamia nuts over the top.

Bake in the preheated oven for about 20–25 minutes until light golden brown and a skewer inserted in the centre comes out just clean. Remove from the oven.

Leave to cool in the tin before removing and cutting into 20 pieces. Store in an airtight container and eat within 4 days.

175 g white chocolate

115 g unsalted butter, diced

100 g caster sugar

2 large eggs, lightly beaten

½ teaspoon vanilla extract

130 g plain flour

½ teaspoon baking powder

150 g macadamia nuts, roughly chopped

100 g white chocolate, roughly chopped or white choc chips

a 23-cm square brownie tin or similar, greased and base-lined

Makes 20

This fruity blondie, made with white chocolate and fresh raspberries, makes a heavenly summer dessert.

white chocolate & raspberry blondies

150 g white chocolate

200 g unsalted butter, diced

3 large eggs

150 g caster sugar

½ teaspoon vanilla extract

200 g plain flour

1 teaspoon baking powder

100 g white chocolate, finely chopped

150 g fresh raspberries

fresh raspberry coulis or sauce, to serve (optional)

a 23-cm square brownie tin or similar, greased and base-lined

Makes 9

Preheat the oven to 180°C (350°F) Gas 4.

Break up the 150 g of white chocolate and put it in a heatproof bowl with the butter and set the bowl over a pan of steaming water. Melt gently, stirring frequently. Do not let the base of the bowl touch the water. Remove the bowl from the pan and set aside until needed.

Break the eggs into a mixing bowl. Use a hand-held electric mixer to whisk until frothy. Add the sugar and vanilla extract and beat thoroughly until very thick and mousse-like in texture.

Whisk in the melted chocolate mixture. Sift the flour and baking powder directly onto the mixture and fold in. Stir in the chopped chocolate. Spoon the mixture into the prepared tin, spread evenly and level the surface. Scatter the fresh raspberries over the top.

Bake in the preheated oven for about 25 minutes or until a skewer inserted in the centre comes out just clean. Remove from the oven.

Leave to cool in the tin before removing and cutting into 9 pieces. Serve with raspberry coulis, if liked. Store in an airtight container and eat within 2 days.

This delicious toffee-flavoured blondie doesn't contain any nuts but if you want to add some, simply replace the dark chocolate with the same weight of walnut halves or chopped Brazil nuts.

butterscotch blondies

115 g unsalted butter

230 g light muscovado sugar

2 large eggs, lightly beaten

½ teaspoon vanilla extract

180 g plain flour

½ teaspoon baking powder

100 g dark chocolate, chopped or dark choc chips

whipped cream, to serve (optional)

a 23-cm square brownie tin or similar, greased and base-lined

Makes 20

Preheat the oven to 180°C (350°F) Gas 4.

Put the butter in a saucepan and melt gently over low heat. Remove the pan from the heat and stir in the sugar with a wooden spoon. Gradually stir in the eggs then the vanilla extract and beat for 1 minute.

Sift the flour and baking powder directly onto the mixture and stir in. Add the chocolate pieces (or nuts if using) and stir until thoroughly combined. Transfer the mixture to the prepared tin, spread evenly and level the surface

Bake in the preheated oven for about 25 minutes until light golden brown and a skewer inserted in the centre comes out just clean. Remove from the oven.

Leave to cool in the tin before removing and cutting into 20 pieces. Serve with a dollop of whipped cream, if liked. Store in an airtight container and eat within 5 days.

Slightly sticky and very chewy, these delicious blondies are heavy with coconut as well as dark and white chocolate. You will need to use the unsweetened type of desiccated coconut.

coconut blondies

Preheat the oven to 180°C (350°F) Gas 4.

Put the coconut in a baking dish and toast in the preheated oven for about 5 minutes, stirring frequently, until a light golden brown. Remove from the oven and set aside to cool. Do not turn off the oven.

Melt the butter in a large saucepan set over low heat. Remove the pan from the heat and stir in the sugar with a wooden spoon. Gradually beat in the eggs then the vanilla extract. Sift the flour and baking powder directly onto the mixture and stir in. Finally, work in the coconut and both the white and dark chopped chocolate. When everything is thoroughly combined transfer the mixture to the prepared tin, spread evenly and level the surface.

Bake in the preheated oven for 20-25 minutes until golden and a skewer inserted in the centre comes out clean. Remove from the oven.

Leave to cool in the tin before removing and cutting into 20 pieces. Serve with a dollop of whipped cream, if liked. Store in an airtight container and eat within 5 days.

175 g desiccated coconut

175 g unsalted butter

300 g light muscovado sugar

2 large eggs, lightly beaten

1 teaspoon vanilla extract

200 g plain flour

1 teaspoon baking powder

50 g white chocolate, chopped, or white choc chips

50 g dark chocolate, chopped, or dark choc chips

whipped cream, to serve (optional)

a 23-cm square brownie tin or similar, greased and base-lined

Makes 20

This is a deliciously moist and chewy little blondie packed with pecan halves, rather than pieces, and flavoured with cinnamon.

cinnamon pecan blondies

Preheat the oven to 180°C (350°F) Gas 4.

Put the butter in a large saucepan set over low heat and melt gently. Add the sugar and cinnamon and stir until smooth and melted. Remove the pan from the heat and set aside to cool for a couple of minutes.

Use a wooden spoon to stir in the eggs, beating the mixture well until thoroughly combined. Sift the flour and baking powder onto the mixture, then stir in. Mix in the pecans then transfer the mixture to the prepared tin, spread evenly and level the surface.

Bake in the preheated oven for about 25 minutes until golden brown and a skewer inserted in the centre comes out just clean. Remove from the oven.

Leave to cool in the tin for 5 minutes before removing and transferring to a wire rack. Wait until it is completely cold before dusting liberally with icing sugar and cutting into 30 small pieces. Store in an airtight container and eat within 4 days.

100 g unsalted butter

300 g light muscovado sugar

½ teaspoon ground cinnamon

2 large eggs, lightly beaten

150 g plain flour

1 teaspoon baking powder

100 g pecan halves

icing sugar, for dusting

a 23-cm square brownie tin or similar, greased and base-lined

Makes 30

Incredibly rich and very moreish! This recipe uses cream cheese instead of butter and then half the mixture is flavoured with white chocolate, the rest with dark chocolate. Walnuts are added at the end to give a contrast in taste and texture.

half blondie, half brownie

Preheat the oven to 180°C (350°F) Gas 4.

Break up the dark chocolate and put it in a heatproof bowl. Set the bowl over a pan of steaming water and melt gently, stirring frequently. Do not let the base of the bowl touch the water. Remove the bowl from the pan and set aside until needed. Melt the white chocolate in the same way and set aside to cool.

Put the cream cheese in a mixing bowl. Add the sugar and use a hand-held electric mixer to beat until smooth. Beat in the eggs, one at a time, then add the vanilla extract. Work in the flour a little at a time on low speed. Transfer half of this mixture to another bowl. Add the melted dark chocolate to one portion and mix thoroughly. Mix the melted white chocolate into the other portion. The dark chocolate mixture will be stiffer than the white.

Using a tablespoon, drop spoonfuls of the dark chocolate mixture into the prepared tin, spacing them evenly apart, with gaps between the blobs. Pour or spoon the white chocolate mixture over the top to fill the spaces. Scatter the nuts over the top. Use the end of a chopstick or the handle of a teaspoon to marble and swirl the two mixtures together.

Bake in the preheated oven for 25–30 minutes until a skewer inserted in the centre comes out just clean. Leave to cool in the tin before removing and cutting into 30 small pieces. Store in an airtight container and eat within 5 days.

100 g dark chocolate

50 g white chocolate

300 g full-fat cream cheese

200 g caster sugar

3 large eggs

1 teaspoon vanilla extract

100 g plain flour

100 g walnut pieces

a 23-cm square brownie tin or similar, greased and base-lined

Makes 30

50 blondies

brownie treats

My children asked for a brownie that could survive life in a school lunchbox. It needed to be nut-free, not too big and, most importantly, not fall apart. I came up with this yummy brownie-style muffin packed with chocolate chips and baked in a paper case. The perfect solution!

brownie 'muffins'

Preheat the oven to 180°C (350°F) Gas 4.

Break the eggs into a mixing bowl, add the sugar and use a hand-held electric mixer or wooden spoon to beat until thoroughly combined. Beat in the melted butter, followed by the milk and the vanilla extract.

Sift the flour, cocoa and baking powder directly onto the mixture and mix in. Finally, stir in the choc chips. Divide the mixture equally between the paper cases and sprinkle a few extra choc chips on the top of each muffin to decorate.

Bake in the preheated oven for about 20-25 minutes until just firm to the touch. (Be aware that these brownies will only rise slightly and won't resemble peaked muffins or cupcakes.)

Remove from the oven and let sit for 5 minutes before transferring to a wire rack to cool completely. Store in an airtight container and eat within 5 days.

2 large eggs

125 g light muscovado sugar

125 g unsalted butter, melted

230 ml full-fat milk

½ teaspoon vanilla extract

225 g plain flour

50 g unsweetened cocoa powder

½ teaspoon baking powder

25 g white choc chips,
plus extra to decorate

25 g dark or milk choc chips,
plus extra to decorate

a 12-cup muffin or cupcake tray, lined with 12 paper cases

Makes 12

Baking a brownie mixture in a crisp pastry case means you can make a very soft, sticky, nutty brownie. This recipe is a family favourite and I always bake it as one of our Thanksgiving pies.

brownie fudge pie

375 g ready-made shortcrust pastry, defrosted if frozen

3 large eggs

150 g light muscovado sugar

150 g dark muscovado sugar

½ teaspoon vanilla extract

175 g unsalted butter, melted

50 g plain flour

50 g unsweetened cocoa powder

150 g pecan halves or pieces

whipped cream, to serve

a 23-cm loose-based tart tin

baking paper

ceramic baking beans or rice

Serves 10

Preheat the oven to 180°C (350°F) Gas 4.

Bring the pastry to room temperature, roll out on a lightly floured surface and use it to line the tart tin. Prick the bottom of the pastry case all over with a fork, line with baking paper and fill with baking beans to weight the paper down. Bake 'blind' in the preheated oven for 12–15 minutes until lightly golden and just firm. Carefully remove the paper and beans and bake for a further 5 minutes until the base is crisp and lightly golden. Remove from the oven and set aside to cool until needed. Do not turn off the oven.

Break the eggs into the bowl of an electric mixer. Whisk until frothy then add the sugar and whisk until very thick and mousse-like in texture. Add the vanilla extract and whisk again to combine. Whisk in the melted butter. Remove the bowl from the mixer and sift the flour and cocoa onto the mixture. Fold in with a large metal spoon. When there are no streaks of flour left, gently stir in the pecans. Transfer the mixture into the cooled pastry case, spread evenly and level the surface. Bake for about 30 minutes or until firm to the touch in the centre. Remove from the oven.

Allow to cool slightly in the tin before removing. Slice and serve warm with whipped cream. Store at room temperature in a covered container and eat within 5 days.

This deliciously gooey brownie pudding is an ideal recipe for absolute beginners. If you have suitable oven to tableware it can be made, baked and served in the same dish so it's a treat for chocolate lovers and washer-uppers alike!

brownie lava pudding

Preheat the oven to 180°C (350°F) Gas 4.

Put the pecan pieces in an ovenproof dish and lightly toast in the preheated oven for about 10 minutes. Set aside until needed. Don't turn the oven off.

Meanwhile break up the chocolate and put it in the flameproof baking dish (or in a saucepan if your baking dish is not flameproof). Add the butter and melt gently over very, very low heat, stirring frequently.

Remove from the heat and stir in the sugar, then gradually stir in the eggs followed by the vanilla.

When thoroughly mixed, stir in the flour and the nuts. When there are no floury streaks scrape down the sides of the dish so that the mixture doesn't scorch. Alternatively, if using a saucepan, transfer the mixture to a buttered baking dish.

Bake in the preheated oven for about 30 minutes until the mixture is set on top with a soft gooey layer at the bottom.

Serve immediately with cream for pouring, or vanilla ice cream.

50 g pecan pieces

100 g dark chocolate

115 g unsalted butter, diced

175 g caster sugar

2 large eggs, lightly beaten

½ teaspoon vanilla extract

75 g plain flour

single cream or vanilla ice cream, to serve

an 18-cm ovenproof baking dish (preferably flameproof too)

Serves 4–6

This special dessert is very easy to prepare using a food processor. The base is a thick, rich, brownie and the topping is a luxuriously deep chocolate cheesecake with pecans.

brownie cheesecake

Preheat the oven to 170°C (325°C) Gas 3.

To make the base, put the butter, sugar, flour and cocoa into the bowl of a food processor and process until the mixture comes together to make a thick paste. Tip this mixture into the prepared tin and press onto the base to make a thick, even layer. Chill while making the topping.

To make the topping, break up the chocolate and put it in a heatproof bowl set over a pan of steaming water. Melt gently, stirring frequently. Do not let the base of the bowl touch the water. Remove the bowl from the pan and stir the chocolate until smooth. Leave for 5 minutes to cool.

Put the cream cheese, eggs, sugar and vanilla extract into the bowl of the food processor. Process until thoroughly combined, scraping down the sides from time to time. With the machine running add the cream through the feed tube, followed by the cooled melted chocolate. When completely combined pour the mixture onto the chilled base, spread evenly and level the surface. Finish by scattering over the pecans.

Stand the tin on a baking tray. Bake in the preheated oven for about 40 minutes until just firm. Turn off the oven but leave the cheesecake inside to cool down, without opening the door. Remove from the oven and chill for at least 4 hours before removing from the tin. Store in an airtight container in the refrigerator and eat within 5 days.

Base:

250 g unsalted butter, chilled and diced

250 g caster sugar

200 g plain flour

50 g unsweetened cocoa powder

Topping:

200 g dark chocolate

400 g full-fat cream cheese

2 large eggs

60 g caster sugar

½ teaspoon vanilla extract

200 ml double cream

50 g pecan halves

a 23–25-cm spring-form tin, greased

Serves 12

Here, a fudgy brownie made with plenty of chocolate and toasted pecans, and baked slightly thinner than usual, is combined with a good shop-bought ice cream – either vanilla or white chocolate works well. Serve with your choice of hot sauce for pouring.

brownie ice cream

Preheat the oven to 180°C (350°F) Gas 4.

To make the brownie mixture, break up the chocolate and put it in a heatproof bowl with the butter. Set over a pan of steaming water and melt gently, stirring frequently. Do not let the base of the bowl touch the water.

Remove the bowl from the pan and use a wooden spoon to stir in the sugar and vanilla extract. Leave to cool for a couple of minutes then stir in the beaten egg.

Sift the flour and cocoa directly onto the mixture then mix in. When thoroughly combined stir in the nuts. Transfer the mixture to the prepared tin and spread evenly.

Bake in the preheated oven for about 12-15 minutes until just firm to the touch. Leave to cool in the tin before removing.

When cool, chop up the brownie into pieces roughly the size of your thumbnail. Transfer the ice cream to the refrigerator to soften (without letting it start to melt) then transfer to a large bowl and mix in the brownie pieces. Spoon into a lidded freezerproof container and freeze until firm.

Serve in scoops with a jug of hot sauce for pouring.

50 g dark chocolate

50 g unsalted butter

100 g light muscovado sugar

½ teaspoon vanilla extract

1 large egg, lightly beaten

50 g plain flour

1½ tablespoons unsweetened cocoa powder

75 g pecan pieces, toasted

750 ml good-quality vanilla or white chocolate ice cream

hot sauce of your choice, to serve (see pages 62–63)

a 23-cm square brownie tin or similar, greased and base-lined

a lidded freezerproof container

Serves 6–8

sauces

chocolate fudge sauce

A lovely thick and rich sauce that's not too sweet.

175 g dark chocolate

40 g unsalted butter, diced

2 tablespoons golden syrup

175 ml single cream

Makes 4–6 servings

Break up the chocolate and put it in a small, heavy-based pan with the butter, golden syrup and cream.

Set over low heat and melt gently, stirring constantly. Continue stirring and heating until the mixture is almost at boiling point. Pour into a warmed jug and serve immediately.

The sauce will thicken as it cools but can be gently reheated.

Any leftover sauce can be covered, stored in the refrigerator for up to 2 days and reheated before use.

butterscotch fudge sauce

A deliciously rich sauce – very good served with any blondie.

90 g unsalted butter, diced

200 g dark muscovado sugar

2 tablespoons golden syrup

90 ml double cream

Makes 6 servings

Put the butter, sugar and golden syrup in a small, heavy-based pan. Melt gently over very low heat, stirring frequently, until the sugar dissolves completely.

When smooth and melted, stir in the cream then increase the heat and stir until the sauce is piping hot but not boiling. Pour into a warmed jug and serve immediately.

Any leftover sauce can be covered, stored in the refrigerator for up to 3 days and reheated before use.

creamy chocolate sauce

A simple yet rich sauce without any added sugar.

125 ml double cream

85 g dark chocolate, chopped

½ teaspoon vanilla extract

Makes 4–6 servings

Pour the cream into a heavy-based saucepan and heat gently, stirring frequently. When the cream comes to the boil remove the pan from the heat and let cool for a minute. Stir in the chopped chocolate and the vanilla extract and keep stirring until smooth. Pour into a warmed jug and serve immediately.

The sauce will thicken as it cools but can be gently reheated.

Any leftover sauce can be covered, stored in the refrigerator for up to 2 days and reheated before use.

white chocolate sauce

Choose good white chocolate flavoured with real vanilla.

200 g white chocolate

200 ml double cream

80 ml milk

1 vanilla pod, split lenghways

Makes 4–6 servings

Break up the chocolate and put it in a heatproof bowl set over a pan of steaming water. Melt gently, stirring frequently. Remove the bowl from the pan and set aside.

Pour the cream and milk into a heavy-based saucepan. Add the vanilla pod and heat, stirring, until scalding hot but not quite boiling.

Remove from the heat and let stand for 5 minutes. Remove the vanilla pod then pour the cream and milk onto the chocolate in a thin stream, whisking constantly, to make a smooth sauce. Pour into a warmed jug and serve immediately.

Any leftover sauce can be covered, stored in the refrigerator for up to 2 days and reheated before use.

coffee sauce

Use good, well-flavoured filter or cafétiere coffee here but not strong espresso.

100 g dark chocolate

60 g unsalted butter, diced

100 ml good coffee

Makes 4–6 servings

Break up the chocolate and put it in a heatproof bowl. Add the butter and coffee then set the bowl over a pan of steaming water.

Let melt gently, stirring frequently, until very smooth. Remove the bowl from the pan and stir until glossy and slightly thickened. As the sauce cools it will become even thicker. Serve warm.

Any leftover sauce can be covered, stored in the refrigerator for up to 2 days and reheated before use.

index

photography credits

All photographs by Richard Jung except:
Peter Cassidy pages 3 background, 4 left,
5, 9, 10, 32, 53, 61, 62 above
Martin Brigdale pages 25, 27, 41
William Reavell pages 23, 24
Tara Fisher page 44
Claire Richardson page 13
Debi Treloar page 21
Polly Wreford page 57